DISCUSSING THE WORD

STUDIES DESIGNED TO PROMOTE DISCUSSION

SATAN'S ASSAULT ON THE FAITH

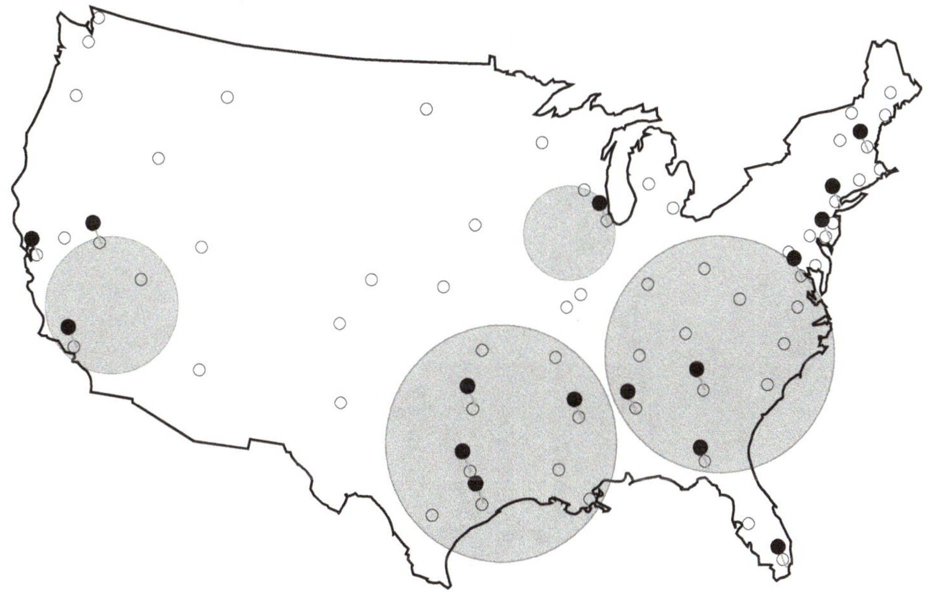

BY CHARLES WILLIS

Printed in the United States of America.

ISBN 10:1-58427-385-2
ISBN 13: 978-1-58427-385-1

Gaurdian of Truth Foundation
CEI Bookstore
220 South Marion Street, Athens, Alabama 35611
1-855-49BOOKS or 1-855-492-6257
www.CEIbooks.com

Table Of Contents

"Finally, be strong in the Lord and in the strength of His might. Put on the full armor of God, so that you will be able to stand firm against the schemes of the devil.... Therefore, take up the full armor of God, so that you will be able to resist in the evil day, and having done everything, to stand firm" (Eph. 6:10-13).

Lesson 1

Satan's Assault On The Faith

EVOLUTION

Can you envision a more successful way of leading people away from God than to convince them that God did not create them? The difference in this lie and the truth of Genesis 1 is just one word. God did NOT create. Just as Eve was seduced when Satan said, "You surely will NOT die" (Gen. 3:4), so men today are deceived by the crafty tale of evolution.

Satan does not present evolution himself. The theory seems logical because the scientists of the world promote it and the science educators teach it. Sadly, even some in the church have been deceived by this lie. Instead of putting trust in the written word of God, men have begun putting their trust and beliefs in the knowledge of men.

In 1859 Charles Darwin published a book entitled *The Origin of Species* in which he put forth his evolutionary beliefs. The book was greeted with great enthusiasm by the scientific community, but not by all. The majority embraced it by faith since there was no evidence to back up the claims of evolution. To this day the THEORY is highly contested in the science community and it continues to undergo change.

Evolution basically describes a process by which new species are developed. It promotes the idea that one species will change over the course of millions of years through mutations that will then arrive at a stable point with no further mutations – thus a new species. For example: an animal with no backbone (invertebrate) mutated multiple times over eons and thus a new species with a backbone (vertebrate) evolved. The problem with this approach is simply that a mutation does not yield a new species. A seedless orange is a mutation, but it is still an orange. Furthermore, a mutation is almost always defective. The seedless orange cannot reproduce without the intervention of man. Mutations are recessive, meaning that successive generations tend to remove the mutation from the animal stock or plant species. The statistical chances of the numerous mutations needed to produce a new species are incalculable to the point it renders the theory of evolution (natural selection) inconceivable.

In Churches of Christ there has been a resurgence of interest in theistic evolution in recent years. This theory promotes the idea that each day of creation consisted of many millions of years. Evolution is asserted to be the method God used to bring about the creation. Theistic evolution is being taught in many so-called "Christian colleges." For many it has become an accepted reality – yet it has no basis in fact. It is mere supposition. It is an attempt to compromise Scripture with the absurd teachings of evolution. It causes some to feel perhaps more "accepted" by the world, but I fear it causes men to be rejected by God. The method God used in bringing about the creation is this: "Then God said…" (Gen. 1:3).

This topic is deserving of deep study and much examination of scientific principles and discoveries. Most of us are not scientists, but the fundamentals are simple in nature and easily understood. It boils down to a simple truth: which requires more faith – a belief in evolution or a belief in God? There is more evidence to believe in God and the creation account; therefore, I believe it takes more faith to believe in evolution. Many do not believe the Genesis account because they have not read it or studied it as they have evolution. Satan is at work in the world convincing men of lies!

Now, Think...

1. The man-discovered "law of biogenesis" states that life comes from life. How would this long established and accepted principle work to refute evolution?

2. What supposed "proofs" of evolution have been put forth in our generation?

3. From Genesis 1 make an argument refuting evolution based on the phrase "after their kind" (vv. 11, 12, 21, 24, 25).

For Discussion

1. Why do people believe the theory of evolution and reject the Genesis account of creation?
2. Why do many who claim to be religious accept theistic evolution as fact?
3. Name three points that convince you evolution is false. These could be points of logic, points of scientific interest, or (especially) passages of Scripture.
4. How has the church suffered by Satan's advancement of evolution?

Satan's Victim

1. Describe Satan's target who is convinced of evolution.
2. What must be done to "un-convince" such a person?

MEDICAL ETHICS

As technology and science advances, Satan confronts the Christian with difficult and, at times, disturbing choices. Many of the issues in this lesson are taken directly from the headlines of the media. They are at the front of our "public discussion." We need to address these questions from the standpoint of Scripture.

ABORTION

The Supreme Court ruled in 1973 that abortion in the first trimester is legal in the United States. In January, 2011, the Guttmacher Institute reported 1.21 million abortions in the US in 2008 (*http://www.numberofabortions.com*, accessed June, 2013). That's 3,315 a day. In Montgomery County, Texas there were 689 abortions performed in 2010 (*http://www.texasalmanac.com/sites/default/files/images/topics/healthcounties14.pdf*, accessed June, 2013). This is almost two abortions every day. The statistics are frightening and depressing.

Are we to suppose that Satan has not influenced some young Christian mother to commit "infanticide" because it is legal in our country? Is the church immune to this national sin? How many of us become truly upset when we think or study about this issue? I fear we have become complacent and accepted this sin as a fact of life in our culture. Rest assured, God does not accept it.

ASSISTED SUICIDE

Rising in competition with abortion (which is generally recognized by believers as wrong) is the concept of an assisted suicide. The lines of right and wrong (in the minds of many believers) are somewhat blurred on this issue. As a society, we have not yet determined if this practice will be accepted or not. Generally it is unacceptable, but attitudes are changing.

What does the Bible teach about suicide? Is it sinful to desire death to the point we take our own life? What about when the life we have left to live is a life of misery due to the ravages of some disease? These issues trouble some folks who claim to believe in Jesus. We must study to know the truth.

CLONING

In January 2008, the U.S. Food and Drug Administration (FDA) approved the sale of cloned animals and their offspring for food (*http://www.scientificamerican.com/article.cfm?id=are-we-eating-cloned-meat*, accessed June, 2013). Like it or not, this is an issue being pushed to the front. It currently involves animals, but it seems only a matter of time before it becomes a matter for humans.

For decades science fiction stories have told of cloned people and cloned societies. A recent Hollywood film (2004) depicted clones who escaped their facility to learn they were "grown" to provide spare parts for the "real" people.

Even closer to reality is the concept of a gay couple or a single mom creating a clone to raise as their child. The technology is in place, but our society and government does not approve. What is the Christian to think? Does God approve or disaprove?

STEM-CELL RESEARCH

Presidet George W. Bush limited stem-cell research in the United States to the existent strains of viable cells (August, 2001). In other words, no new stem-cells are harvested legally in this country, but they are in other countries. They are taken from aborted babies. These cells have the ability to adapt into any other cell in the body which gives the potential for regenerating disease-ridden bodies back to health.

Doctors are excited about the prospects and are pushing the research forward as quickly as possible. What is the Christian to think? Must we decline a new medical "miracle" to save our lives if it has been developed from aborted babies?

These issues (and many more) are facing Christians in the field of medicine. I hope that studying the following passages will aid in our understanding of God's will and help us remain faithful in His sight. We all need to study these things.

Now, Think...

1. Why is abortion sinful (Exod. 21:22-24; Gen. 25:22; Jer. 1:5; Ps. 139:13-16; Rom. 13:9)?

2. Why would a woman want an abortion?

3. What does the Bible reveal about suicide?

   A. Examples of suicide: Judges 16:29-30; 1 Samuel 31:4-5; 2 Samuel 17:23; 1 Kings 16:18; Matthew 27:5 and Acts 1:18.

   B. Consider also Matthew 4:5-7.

   C. Is suicide condemned?

4. Is assisted suicide sinful (Exod. 20:13; Eph. 6:2; 1 Tim. 5:4, 8)?

Satan's Victim

1. What logic is used to promote a worldly attitude toward abortion instead of a spiritual outlook?

2. Who is most likely to give in to Satan's logic and temptation about some of these issues?

For Discussion

1. Compare God's attitude toward parents who sacrificed their children to an idol with those who abort their children today (see Lev. 20:2-5; Jer. 32:35).

2. Is assisted suicide the same as removing a person from life-sustaining equipment that the person may die "naturally"?

3. How did God deal with Jonah's wish to die (Jonah 4:3, 8-9)?

4. Should Christians accept medical treatment that has been created through a sinful means (i.e., aborted babies)? Why or why not (see 1 Thess. 5:22)?

5. What are the results of accepting Satan's attack in the area of medical ethics? Where will it lead us?

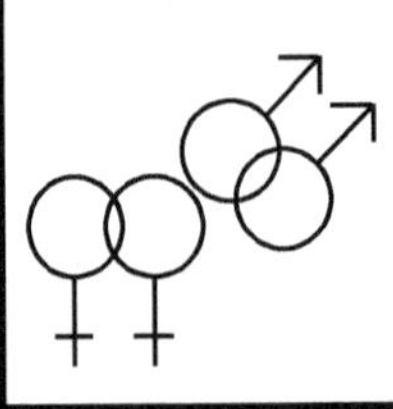

Lesson 3

Satan's Assault On The Faith

HOMOSEXUALITY & GAY MARRIAGE

While I understand that a discussion of such a topic can be disgusting, it nevertheless needs to be discussed. We are assaulted on a daily basis by the homosexual agenda in our country. This movement has been at work the last 25 years to promote an acceptance of this sin in the eyes of the general population. Sadly, to a large extent, they are succeeding.

On a regular basis, television programming includes homosexual and lesbian characters. They are portrayed as wholesome, accepted, and not controversial to the other characters. Many of the Hollywood elite have "come out of the closet" to admit their sin. While the agenda of the homosexual movement has succeeded in promoting an open discussion and general acceptance in the society, they are not satisfied with stopping there.

Many new social issues are being forced upon the population by this grossly small minority group. State governments have adopted some sort of policy toward "gay marriage," either pro or con. In June of 2013, the Supreme Court ruled the national Defense of Marriage Act unconstitutional which forces government institutions to provide marital benefits to married homosexual couples. Gay marriage is a reality.

Beyond this is the concept of "gay adoption." Homosexual and lesbian couples are beginning to adopt children into their homes. While I do not deny they can have love for a child, it is detrimental to the child to live in a house with such decadently sinful behavior being flaunted. They will most likely grow up to themselves become sexually sinful in one way or another. The adoption agencies and state agencies are beginning to view such "families" as acceptable, and this is greatly alarming!

The question for the children of God is this: will we continue to stand against this sin as our society accepts it? It appears many countries in the world are beginning to accept this unnatural behavior, but God does not and neither should the Christian. It could well be argued that our own country worked hard in years past to outlaw drinking, gambling, pornography, and whoredom – yet all of those things are now accepted.

Many in the church do not feel gambling is sinful or that an occasional drink is sinful. Will we "grow" to accept the sin of homosexuality?

With the advances of this behavior in the last 25 years, it is terrible to consider where we will be in another 25 years. What legal ramifications will come from the nation's acceptance of this sin? What persecutions will be brought against the faithful for opposing it? Will we continue to fight? Only if our children are taught the truth today! Only if we ourselves are committed to standing for the truth.

Satan is strongly at work in our country. Homosexuality is not a new sin – it has been around since biblical times, condemned by God in Sodom and Gomorrah. Satan continues to promote among men an acceptance of what God hates. It worked in the Roman world – one of the main reasons that nation fell apart was because of a breakdown of the family unit. They were consumed with sinful sexual behavior even worse than presently exists in our nation. Satan would love nothing more than to tear down this nation that is supposedly built on "Christian ethics," and to destroy the Lord's church that is strongly opposing sin of any kind. The breakdown of the family just may be the inroad that will work for him. We must be diligent and watchful to overcome his trickery.

Now, Think...

1. From Romans 1:26-27, make a list of the words describing the sin of homosexuality.

2. Why was Sodom destroyed?

   A. What was the sin (Gen. 19:5)?

   B. How is this described in 2 Peter 2:6-8; Jude 7; Matthew 11:23-24; Luke 17:29?

3. What was God's attitude about this sin in Leviticus 20:13?

4. How does Jesus teach on this matter in Matthew 19:4-6?

For Discussion

1. Read 1 Corinthians 6:9-11.
   A. What sexual sins are spoken of?

   B. How can we use this text to argue against a "homosexual religious leader"?

   C. What changed for these people that allowed them to be justified?

2. Can a person involved in a homosexual relationship remain in the relationship and please God? In other words, is there such a thing as a "homosexual Christian"? (Give scriptural justification for your answer other than 1 Cor. 6:11.)

3. Satan is working hard to influence the faithful. What would be the result of one generation of Christians accepting this sin and continuing to worship God in truth (in all other ways)?

   A. Have similar things happened in the past?

   B. How were things "corrected"?

Satan's Victim

1. Describe the adult who will accept or participate in this sin. Who is Satan targeting?

2. How can such persons be convinced of his/her sin?

Lesson 4 Satan's Assault On The Faith

ENTERTAINMENT versus WORSHIP

It happened in my own back yard - Houston, Texas. The largest mega–church in the Country opened in 2006. Lakewood Church held a "Grand Opening" at their new facility – the old Compaq Center, which had been a sports arena. At the "Grand Opening" event, more than 57,000 people attended and they had to turn people away to avoid breaking the fire-code laws. This "event" was broadcast live on two television networks worldwide.

Joel Osteen and the Lakewood Church epitomize much of the "new" in religious thinking today. Their worship assemblies are broadcast weekly on television. Their facility renovation cost $95 million in addition to the 50-year lease agreement. Marketing of Lakewood Church is seen all over the Houston, Texas area on billboards, papers, magazines, the Internet, and television. Their "image" is very important, and the smiling Joel Osteen with open arms and up-turned hands is almost a trademark. Most of the religious world calls this a great success.

Sadly, that cannot be what God thinks. Mr. Osteen has admitted his preaching focuses on "the goodness of God" rather than discussing sin (*www.foxnews.com/story/0,2933,110240,00.html*, accessed June, 2013). The music is "contemporary" (meaning it sounds like pop radio music) and the lessons are high tech. Many who have gone to Lakewood Church in the past have told me that the lessons are lacking in content and depth. It's all about "feeling good." That is exactly the method of modern worship in mega-churches.

The focus in such worship assemblies has shifted away from God and focuses on the individual. Rather than being about "worship" it is about "entertainment." Rather than singing as a congregation, groups listen to praise bands and choirs. You don't see these groups partaking of the Lord's Supper – except perhaps at Christmas and Easter (when it is politically correct to do so as a church that supposedly follows Christ).

Emotions run high in these entertaining events. They are designed to create that emotional reaction. They want people to get "pumped up" by the music. They want people to "cry with tears" at the videos. They want folks to "feel" as if they have been "moved" by the experience. There is nothing wrong with emotion in a worship assembly – but to arouse emotional responses is not the purpose of worship. That's what has been missed so greatly – people have forgotten why we worship.

There is even a trend among groups that call themselves a "Church of Christ" to adopt some of the techniques and methods of the mega-churches. Must we follow the trend toward entertainment in order for people to learn the truth of God? I think not. How entertaining was the teaching of Jesus or the apostles? Was that their purpose? Surely, hopefully, we can see this is terribly wrong.

Satan has again concocted a method to draw people away from God. They believe they are serving Him, when in fact they are not pleasing Him. Entertainment only benefits *us* – it does not benefit God. God did not send His Son to die on the cross so we could be entertained. Satan's success is growing. We need to be observant and wise in seeing his evil ploys. He seeks to deceive us. Many do not know that they have already been devoured by him. Entertainment as "worship" is a work of the devil and we should have no part in it.

Now, Think...

1. From Matthew 7:21-23, state the error of "mega-churches."

2. What did the church do when they gathered together? (Acts 2:42) How might this be used to refute the "new tradition" of entertainment?

3. Give reasons why fundraising is not scriptural (example: selling recordings of music by the "church band").

4. What is the proper demeanor of one who is worshipping (see John 4:24; 1 Cor. 11:27-29; 14:15, 40)?

For Discussion

1. What is scripturally wrong with "giving people what they want" in a worship service (2 Tim. 4:2-3)?

2. What is the "drawing power" of a mega-church? What *should* cause folks to attend a worship assembly? Is this a problem in the Lord's church?

3. Are those in the worship assembly supposed to be spectators or participants? (Give biblical support for your answer.)

4. Does the concept of a "mega-church" violate the great commission (Matt. 28:18-20)?

5. In the emotional events of a mega-church worship assembly what has been 'lost sight of' (Matt. 4:10)?

6. How has Satan succeeded in drawing people away from God?

Satan's Victim

1. What are participants of a mega-church "looking" for? What have they found that they like?

2. Who in the Lord's church might be drawn away by such a group?

Lesson 5 Satan's Assault On The Faith

A LACK OF DISCIPLINE IN THE CHURCH

A major problem in many local churches today is a failure to follow the commands of God in regard to discipline. Both individuals and congregations have elected to ignore these instructions, and that decision only leads to problems. What we must understand is that a failure to follow any command of God will result in our condemnation. Scripture has a lot to say on the subject of discipline and we need to hear it all.

First let's consider an individual's responsibility. We have God-given obligations to our fellow saints. They are not optional, though many ignore them. "Even if anyone is caught in any trespass, you who are spiritual, restore such a one in a spirit of gentleness; each one looking to yourself, so that you too will not be tempted. Bear one another's burdens, and thereby fulfill the law of Christ" (Gal. 6:1-2). The "spiritual" Christian is another way of speaking of the mature. The weak, young, and immature Christians are not given this instruction. Each of us must personally decide if the passage applies to us. Those who are living righteously and faithful unto God are instructed to restore the erring brother or sister. In the questions that follow, the scriptural process we are to follow in restoring one will be further examined; however, we do need to understand the attitude and demeanor God commanded one to have when restoring an erring brother. A spirit of gentleness must prevail. Too often a spirit of anger, discouragement, or disgust may prevail – and this is wrong.

Secondly, let's consider the congregation's responsibility. It is sad but true that some congregations have not "practiced" discipline in decades. It is not a problem from a lack of knowledge – most of these goups know the passages and at times even teach on the subject. The problem is in application. There are two concepts involved in congregational discipline. We are to "keep away [withdraw – King James] from every brother who leads an unruly life" (2 Thess. 3:6). We also read that we are to "mark" them that are causing divisions and occasions of stumbling (Rom.16:17). Withdrawing and marking are concepts that must be understood and followed by every congregation that desires to please God.

Elders are to lead a congregation and watch for the flock. It is, therefore, imperative that elders lead in exercising discipline. The problem for many elders is in exercising good wisdom in regard to individuals. God has not given us "cut-and-dried" instructions about exactly when discipline should begin or end. We must rely on the judgment of wise elders. For example: when does a person move out of the realm of a struggling believer to one who is walking disorderly? Wisdom is greatly needed. But to *never* discipline will only lead to more disorder. It can even allow some to believe they are righteous when they are not.

The importance of discipline cannot be overstated, but from the way it is often neglected, some appear to believe it is not important at all. This is a sad situation when many, even of the Lord's congregations, are not following His law. Satan must be smiling! Have we learned nothing from the mistakes of the Israelites?

Now, Think...

1. What process does Scripture teach for the individual approaching a fellow saint who is in error (James 5:19; Gal. 6:1; Matt. 18:15)? How is this done incorrectly?

2. What process does Scripture teach for the congregation in dealing with an erring saint (Matt. 18:16-17; 1 Cor. 5:4-13)? How is this done incorrectly?

3. What specifics are given as reasons for withdrawing and marking? (1 Tim. 1:19-20; Gal. 6:1; 2 Thess. 3:14; Rom. 16:17-18; Titus 3:10; 1 Cor. 5:1-13; 1 Tim. 5:20)

For Discussion

1. Is it wrong for elders to exercise discipline without involving the congregation? (1 Cor. 5:4; 1 Tim. 5:20; 2 Thess. 3:6)

2. What should be our behavior and attitude toward those withdrawn from? (2 Thess. 3:14-15; 1 Cor. 5:1-13; Titus 3:10-11)

3. What is the purpose of congregational discipline? (1 Cor. 5:5-6; Gal. 6:1-2)

4. What are the results of ignoring these passages and not practicing discipline (both individual and congregational)?

Satan's Victim

1. What is the mind-set of one who would ignore such strong teaching in Scripture?

2. Why are some unwilling to begin practicing this godly doctrine?

CHURCH DISCIPLINE
Forgotten Doctrine of the 21st Century

Lesson 6

Satan's Assault On The Faith

WEAK PREACHING & TEACHING

The nature of religious teaching has undergone a dramatic shift in recent decades. The emphasis is no longer on what the Bible says, but instead is on presenting a message in such a way that it is palatable. This trend has even found residence within the Lord's church. This "easier to hear teaching" is what I am calling "weak preaching."

Paul, in writing about the apostles, said, "We preach Christ crucified, to Jews a stumbling block and to Gentiles foolishness, but to those who are the called, both Jews and Greeks, Christ the power of God and the wisdom of God" (1 Cor. 1:23-24). The purpose of preaching is to teach men about Jesus, the Christ who was crucified. When we can understand Jesus is the Messiah come from heaven to die on the cross for our sins, we are motivated to live for God. "How will they hear without a preacher?" (Rom. 10:14). From the beginning it has been God's plan "through the foolishness of the message preached to save those who believe" (1 Cor. 1:21). We need preachers in the church who are part of God's plan in bringing the message of salvation. The church does not need men who are unwilling to preach truth and who instead bring a palatable message.

Many who preach in denominations and in other religious groups have begun to preach lessons that are devoid of any substantial content. Their "feel good" message is appealing to many, but it is not always truth and certainly does not teach a person how to become mature and full of faith. Even in the Lord's body there is a decided *lack* of spiritual knowledge. Weak preaching and teaching has done much to undermine the sure foundation of the faith of many. How else could so many Christians be led into error that was doctrinally clear only 40 or 50 years ago? Not all blame can be ascribed to teachers and preachers – but they have surely contributed to many having a weak faith. That is the result of weak preaching – weak faith.

Many preachers would never dream of bringing a series of lessons such as we read in 1 Corinthians. To specifically address congregational problems, to teach the truth in a "take it or leave it" style. To present it boldly regardless of whether men find it palatable. This direct teaching has become unacceptable for many. As we examine Scripture, we do not see weak preaching converting the world, but bold, blunt, straight forward preaching that was understood. This kind of preaching and teaching instilled great faith in the hearts of the listeners who were severely persecuted in the first century.

The times of Malachi appear to be re-visiting us when God's message has been polluted by men who will not teach truth. Partial truth will not build faith in God's word. To willfully not preach on Bible subjects, to willfully ignore congregational problems – these things only open the door for saints to lose their faith or be led astray. Preaching all truth is again thought of as foolishness for it does not attract many – only those who desire truth and righteousness before God. We must never relinquish God's trust to us in preaching the gospel. It is the power of God unto salvation (Rom. 1:16). No more effective method of tearing down the church has ever been devised by Satan than weak preaching!

Now, Think...

1. What instructions are given to the preacher (2 Tim. 2:2; 4:2; Titus 2:15)

2. What is the proper attitude of an evangelist (2 Tim. 2:23-25; 4:2)?

3. Where should preaching be done (Acts 5:42)?

For Discussion

1. Read Galatians 1:10. How do some preachers in the Lord's body seek the favor of men?

2. Who does a preacher work for: elders, God, or the congregation?

3. What are preachers supposed to preach about?

   A. Galatians 1:8-9

   B. Ephesians 4:15

   C. Mark 16:15-16

   D. 2 Timothy 1:13-14

   E. Titus 1:10-13

   F. 1 Timothy 6:17-19

   G. 1 Timothy 4:6

   H. 1 Timothy 4:13

Satan's Victim

1. What would cause a man to be classed as a weak preacher or teacher?

2. Do weak preachers and teachers know they are "weak"?

3. Must one remain a weak preacher or teacher?

Lesson 7 Satan's Assault On The Faith

ELDERS WHO FOLLOW

& THOSE WHO DON'T WANT ELDERS

There is a real problem in the church that threatens to undermine and destroy her. This situation must be a result of Satan's actions. He has attacked the organization of the church yet again. In years past, this ploy has proven to be successful for Satan, leading to the development of the Catholic Church, denominationalism, and even the modern trend of "fellowship" and "community" churches. You would think God's people could recognize another attack in this area – but Satan has been subtle. We will pursue two areas in this lesson.

First, elders who follow. It is only natural, that in any group of men, the tendency will be to see one as a leader whom the others follow. That is NOT God's plan for the eldership. God insists there be multiple elders in every congregation (Acts 14:23). This organization prevents dictatorships, where one man could lead a congregation into error. But when elders look to a single elder and FOLLOW him – they have essentially removed God's plan. They become elders in name only. Elders who rule well are deserving of double honor (1 Tim. 5:17), but the lone elder who takes the lead only complicates God's plan. When elders fail to independently evaluate situations and decisions, when they fail to truly be involved – only problems will result. Truth will be seldom upheld. Failures in discipline will occur. Things will be done without the knowledge or approval of other elders. We don't need elders who follow men – we need elders who follow Christ and God's written word!

Second, consider that some do not desire elders today. A later lesson in this book will discuss a lack of godly men (due to lack of knowledge) that reduces the number of men qualified to serve as elders. This lesson will examine those who are perfectly content in a congregation without elders. In such a case there is no plan for gaining elders in the future. We hear some say: the business meetings are working fine – we don't really need elders. I strongly disagree! We DO need elders because God says we do. This attitude simply endorses a departure from God's plan for organizing the church. It is heretical, wrong, and sinful. Yet it exists and is growing among the Lord's people. It is an accepted idea in many small, "out-of-the-way" congregations that have no elders.

Many do not recognize the assault of Satan on the Faith. They read of him in Scripture but are not alert and watchful for him. Because of this, some are being led into error, or at least have wrong ideas about what God finds acceptable. Let me emphasize, I am not saying it is wrong or sinful for a congregation to be without elders – but that this arrangement should not be permanent or preferred. Unqualified men as elders also introduce problems about which we are warned in Scripture. Satan's ways work. They have been successful in the past. He keeps using them. Let us be mindful, observant, and dedicated to God's ways.

Now, Think...

1. What instructions are given in Scripture to prevent someone from being a "head" elder (1 Tim. 3:6-7; Titus 1:7-8; 1 Pet. 5:1-3)?

2. What instructions are given about the saints' obligations and attitudes toward Elders (Heb. 13:17; 1 Tim. 5:17-19)?

Satan's Victim

1. What is the mind-set of the elder who "follows"?

2. What kind of believers prefer to worship in a congregation without elders?

For Discussion

1. How long should a congregation wait before electing to the eldership a mature man who has only recently identified? Why?

2. Scripture requires a plurality of elders. Why do most congregations seem to prefer three or more?

3. What problems arise from an eldership comprised of a leader and follower(s)?

4. What blessings come from an eldership composed of leaders?

5. What problems arise in congregations without elders?

Lesson 8

Satan's Assault On The Faith

INDIFFERENCE

Since the creation, Satan has not ceased to attack us through the avenue of indifference. This problem is simply an attitude of 'unconcern.' Many who truly believe in God are unconcerned about some particulars in their lives. Congregations suffer when indifference is the general attitude.

Jesus said it best when addressing the church in Laodicea, "I know your deeds, that you are neither cold nor hot; I wish that you were cold or hot. So because you are lukewarm, and neither hot nor cold, I will spit you out of My mouth" (Rev. 3:15-16). This text speaks of indifference as demonstrated in deeds. The saints were not hot, meaning they were not zealous (v.19), nor were they cold, meaning they were doing nothing. They were in-between, and their indifference lay in their lack of concern that they were in sin. Jesus instructed them to "be zealous and repent" (v.19). God has never been pleased with half-hearted devotion.

Those who have allowed indifference to develop in their hearts do not realize they are in danger. There is a need to repent and become zealous as God expects. A callous attitude that is unconcerned about sin is only a short step away from giving up entirely and returning to the ways of the world. If there is no concern over sin now, why should we expect to be concerned about it in the future? This attitude is deceptively dangerous because we think we are doing alright in our service – we convince ourselves of it by thinking, "I'm doing enough." This is especially true when other Christians have developed indifference. We then think we are "normal" and "right" in our attitude. Jesus says he would spit us out.

He would rather we be hot (zealous), as He demands in verse 19, or cold (doing nothing). How can He prefer that we be cold? If we were doing nothing we could be convinced of our error, we would be more likely to repent, but as we are lukewarm we must work harder to see the need to repent. Certainly we must understand Jesus is not pleased with an indifferent attitude.

How many times do we read about the Israelites offering sacrifices at the high places? God condemns this over and over, yet the people continue to go back to the high places. Even if they were offering their sacrifices to Jehovah in these places – God still indicates it was wrong. One of the main distinctions between a "good" king and a "bad" king in the Israelite nation was whether or not he tore down the high places. Can we not learn from their indifference to God's law? It was an uncaring attitude that continued to grow to the point they were worshipping idols and God. They were happy to embrace the cultures around them and adopt their ways along with God's ways. God allowed the Northern Kingdom and eventually the Southern Kingdom to be taken into captivity because of a sorry attitude. Only then did they seem to have remorse over their sin.

Saints in the Lord's church are plagued with an attitude of indifference. If we were zealous – oh, what marvelous things could be accomplished. Instead, in many congregations, the struggle for righteousness is largely comprised of the few zealous ones struggling to encourage the many who are indifferent so that they will not completely turn their back on God. Is it not true that in most congregations a righteous few are very busy doing God's work and the majority simply "attend assemblies"? We need to heed the warning of Christ in Revelation 3 to be zealous and repent. An indifferent attitude does not please God, it pleases Satan.

Now, Think...

1. What words are used to describe the indifference of Gallio? (Acts 18:12-16)

2. What does Jesus teach about indifference in Luke 10:30-32?

3. Of what were the Pharisees indifferent in Matthew 27:3-4?

For Discussion

For each of the following, describe (1) how we can be indifferent, (2) how that indifference effects the congregation, and (3) what God's word says that should cause us to be zealous.

1. Indifference about worship.
2. Indifference about personal growth.
3. Indifference about edifying the saints.
4. Indifference about loving one another.
5. Indifference about teaching others.
6. Indifference about serving others.
7. Indifference about doctrine.

Satan's Victim

1. How does a person develop an indifferent attitude?
2. How does a person change his/her attitude to being zealous?

WARNING!
Adult content,
you must be
at least 18 years old
to enter this site.

Lesson 9

Satan's Assault On The Faith

PORNOGRAPHY

Less than one mile from the church building is a convenience store that sells pornography. Are you shocked? Probably not. We've grown accustomed to the availability of viewing naked people. It is promoted as "fun," "entertaining," and "harmless." It is none of these. Viewing pornography is sin.

No one can deny that the purpose of looking at naked people is to create and enjoy lustful thoughts. Jesus condemns this very behavior in Matthew 5:28. It is a mental romp through the gutter of sin – but just because we are not physically involved does not mean it is not sinful.

What follows are some statistics gathered from *Familysafemedia.com.* They are accurate as of 2006.

- Pornography is a $57 billion industry worldwide – $12 Billion in the U.S.
- Porn revenue is larger than all the revenue from all the professional football, baseball, and basketball teams combined.
- 12% of all Internet sites are pornographic (4.2 million).
- 25% of all Internet search engine requests (68 million) are pornographic.
- 47% of "Christians" said pornography is a major problem in their home.
- Visitors to pornographic websites are men (72%) and women (28%).
- 9.4 million women access adult websites every month.
- 100,000 websites offer illegal child pornography.
- There are 116,000 requests DAILY for child pornography.
- 20% of youth have received a sexual solicitation on-line.
- 89% of youth in chat-rooms receive a sexual solicitation.

There are currently many books, websites, and even professional physcologists that deal solely with the behavioral problem called "sexual addiction." THE major component that leads to the uncontrolled behavior is viewing of pornographic material. Many are unwilling to admit or are unaware that they have a problem.

The so-called "soft porn" market is booming on premium cable television. If we subscribe to them (HBO, Cinemax, Showtime, etc.) we must understand the pornographic programming is included. Hotels regularly offer pay-per-view pornography. We must not blind ourselves and think this is not a problem that affects some who desire to be right with God. This is a sin to which Christians fall. Satan must love Hollywood and the pornographic producers.

Viewing pornography would have to be considered a secret sin. Most who participate, especially those who have a "sexual addiction," are known for keeping this a secret even from their spouse. One of the first steps to "recovery" is to admit the addiction to a friend. There are many services available that disclose your Internet website visits to an approved friend to promote accountability. But we must not forget that God sees all that we do. There is no secret sin with God. We need to repent (if involved) and remember we will be held accountable by God!

The Bible has much to say about nakedness and viewing it, which will be examined below. I urge everyone to understand God's attitudes and teaching on this sin and remember the judgment day is coming. Satan must love the abuses mankind has made of the Internet. Let us pray that we do not get pulled into his trap of pornography.

Satan's Victim

1. What would cause a person to visit an Internet pornography site?

2. What is necessary to change this behavior?

Now Think...

1. What has been God's attitude about nakedness in the past?
   A. Isaiah 20:4

   B. Exodus 28:42-43

   C. Exodus 20:26

   D. Leviticus 18:6-19

   E. Genesis 9:20-25

2. What is God's attitude about nakedness now? (1 Tim. 2:9)

For Discussion

1. What things are Christians supposed to seek? (Phil. 4:8) How do these combat viewing pornography?

2. From the works of the flesh (Gal. 5:18-21) list those that are promoted or condoned by pornography.

3. What should be the attitude of the Christian? (1 Thess. 5:2)

4. Relate the importance of these two passages in regard to pornography. How do we obey them?
   A. 2 Corinthians 10:5

   B. Job 31:1

Lesson 10

Satan's Assault On The Faith

WOLVES IN OUR MIDST

Paul told the Ephesian elders, "I know that after my departure savage wolves will come in among you, not sparing the flock; and from among your own selves men will arise, speaking perverse things, to draw away the disciples after them" (Acts 20:29-30). Departure from the truth has always been led by a false teacher from our midst who convinces some to follow him. History confirms this truth through an examination of the rise of Catholicism.

In my parents' generation, there was rise of a false doctrine that divided many congregations across the country. It focused on the work of one congregation in Abilene, Texas, to host a national radio program titled "The Herald of Truth." A number of debates and public discussions within congregations resulted from a departure from the doctrine of Christ. Many groups today who call themselves a "Church of Christ" actively support institutions of men from their treasury (colleges, missionary societies, children's homes, hospitals, etc.). This departure from truth was led by men who were trusted and considered to be knowledgable about Scripture.

Satan's assault on the faith through a false teacher in our midst continues in our time. Edward Fudge led a departure from the truth. A graduate of Florida College in the 1960s, Mr. Fudge now attends with the Bering Drive Church of Christ in Houston, Texas. His book, *The Fire That Consumes*, sets forth his position that there is no hell, but that the sinner upon dying passes into oblivion and is annihilated. His work has been praised among many denominations and some groups calling themselves a "Church of Christ." This is a man who arose from our midst speaking perverse things.

There have been many men from our midst who have been speaking perverse things. Their doctrines should trouble us greatly because they are not the doctrine of Christ, and we know those who accept and promote them do not have the Father or the Son (2 John 9). From our midst have come false teachings about divorce and remarriage, the days of creation, the social gospel, sponsoring church arrangements, and the teaching that Christ returned in A.D. 70 ("realized eschatology"). Many other teachings arise that do not gain a broad, national awareness; however, men are still led astray by a wolf.

The wolf in the midst can be more readily found amoung groups that have already accepted institutionalism and the social gospel as the push for departure from Christ's doctrine is more apparent and forceful. Men are following these false teachers and accepting their false doctrines, which will result in the loss of their souls. Open fellowship with denominations is practiced. They consider people in denominations to be brothers and sisters "in Christ," even though they were not "baptized into Christ" (Gal. 3:27). This practice is a result of a doctrine that claims baptism is not necessary, but is merely our tradition. Instruments of music in worship are being accepted by many groups. Women are accepted in the church organization and in leadership during worship assemblies. How did men come to accept doctrines so far removed from Scripture? It was a wolf in their midst.

We are foolish to think this departure will not happen again. "But false prophets arose among the people, just as there will also be false teachers among you, who will secretly introduce destructive heresies, even denying the Master who bought them, bringing swift destruction upon themselves. Many will follow their sensuality, and because of them the way of the truth will be maligned" (2 Pet. 2:1-2). Wolves arise from our midst and we have a responsibility to uphold the truth of God while defeating the false teacher. This is the purpose of the Lord's church, to be "the pillar and support of the truth" (1 Tim. 3:15). While elders bear the load of this responsibility (Titus 1:9), it is a responsibility of every Christian as a member of the church. This is especially true when the wolf in our midst is a preacher or elder. Faithful men and women are needed to stand for the truth.

It becomes difficult when we realize the wolf in our midst is a friend – someone we have perhaps worshipped with for years. To stand opposed will result in a loss of friendship, and many are not willing. Our clarity of thinking is already muddled in that we would rather remain the friend of the false teacher than be the friend of God. Let us study diligently to show ourselves approved unto God, that we might be able to recognize the wolf in our midst and keep ourselves pure and spotless for the day of Christ's return. Most assuredly, Satan is assaulting us with false teachers.

Now, Think...

1. What passage(s) teach we are not to follow men, but God's word?

2. Give two references describing a false teacher.

For Discussion

1. Give scriptural evidence proving the error of each point.
   A. Pulpit swaps with denominations.

   B. The church is just another denomination.

   C. A lack of scriptural prohibition grants authority for the practice.

   D. Baptism is a demonstration of our trust in Jesus, but it does not save us.

   E. There's nothing wrong with women ministers.

   F. The unrighteous will not be tortured forever. A loving God allows them to pass into oblivion.

2. What does Scripture reveal about how we are to refute false doctrine (consider 1 John 4:1; 1 Pet. 3:15-16)?

Satan's Victim

1. Who is likely to follow a false teacher?

2. What mind-set must exist in those who promote false doctrine?

Lesson 11 **Satan's Assault On The Faith**

BITING & DEVOURING ONE ANOTHER

Of all the strategies of Satan intended to cause men to lose faith, none has been more successful than the discouragement derived from disputes among brethren. This is a serious problem that many are unwilling to admit. Some brethren only seem to be happy when contentions are present.

"For the whole Law is fulfilled in one word, in the statement, 'You shall love your neighbor as yourself.' But if you bite and devour one another, take care that you are not consumed by one another" (Gal. 5:14-15). God's desire is for our love to be apparent and reigning, rather than contentions. The danger of bickering is that we may be consumed. How many have you known who left the faith, or left a congregation, because men could not behave in a loving fashion? Too many in my experience. In general, the non-institutional congregations calling themselves a "Church of Christ" have splintered themselves into small groups as a result of biting and devouring attitudes. The majority of congregations are below 100 in attendance and groups over 200 are rare.

There are many important passages that teach what Christian attitudes and behaviors toward each other ought to be, yet the problem (the sin) still continues. Jesus instructs us to "be at peace with one another" (Mark 9:50), which Paul repeats saying brethren are to "live in peace" (2 Cor. 13:11; 1 Thess. 5:13). Nevertheless, in the writings of the New Testament it is obvious that problems plagued brethren over words, strife, contentions, quarrels, bitterness, and more. We still struggle with these things, but that does not excuse our choosing sinful behavior. Rather, it brings to the forefront our continued need to improve and carefully cherish our relationships with each other.

There are many reasons brethren continue to fail to live at peace with one another. None seems more apparent than opinions being doggedly held as doctrine. Opinions that do not conflict with divine revelation are fine for us to personally hold, and we even are told to not violate our conscience (Rom. 14:5, 23). The problem is when we want to bind them on others (when God has not). We begin to view one who does not hold our opinion with contempt (Rom. 14:3) and judge each other as condemned before God (Rom. 14:10). In so doing we place "stumbling blocks" before each other (Rom. 14:13; 1 Cor. 8:9) and can be guilty of causing a brother to sin (Rom. 14:23), which is sin for us (1 Cor. 8:11-12). This attitude of teaching opinion as truth has indeed been a stumbling block to some who have since left the Lord. It has led congregations to division.

Brotherly love is to be the governing attitude among Christians. By this men will know we are disciples of Christ (John 13:35). God has taught us to "love one another" (1 Thess. 4:9), yet we at times prefer to exhibit unloving behavior and attitudes. The willingness to forgive is not as apparent as the willingness to accuse and attack. Gentleness in speech is at times lacking. Consideration, tact, and politeness are used among non-believers, but within the family of God such loving courtesies are often forgotten. Sibling bickering rises up and quickly results in harsh feelings. "See to it that no one comes short of the grace of God; that no root of bitterness springing up causes trouble, and by it many be defiled" (Heb. 12:15). When bitterness exists between two brethren, many others can be drawn into the contention and thereby defiled. Look how far removed we are from "let love of the brethren continue" (Heb. 13:1).

Satan loves nothing more than to see congregations in upheaval. Every Christian should contend for the truth – it is an expectation of God. Most congregations today (where unrest exists) have problems with brethren who enjoy stirring up strife and/or teaching opinions that are bound on others. Until we acknowledge our sin and repent, Satan will continue to be pleased with our biting and devouring one another.

Satan's Victim

1. What sentiments and attitudes cause a Christian to bite and devour another?

2. How can such a person change in order to please God? What must change?

Now, Think...

1. What principles are taught in 1 John 4:7-21 regarding our attitude toward brethren?

2. What is the source of quarrels and conflicts (James 4:1-2)?

3. What does it mean to be "devoted to one another in brotherly love" (Rom. 12:10)?

For Discussion

Examine each passage relating it to biting and devouring. Make a list of points you would emphasize in each passage.

1. Proverbs 26:20-28

2. Ephesians 4:29-32

3. 1 Peter 3:8-12

4. Colossians 3:12-14

Lesson 12

Satan's Assault On The Faith

A LACK OF KNOWLEDGE

"My people go into exile for their lack of knowledge" (Isa. 5:13).
"My people are destroyed for lack of knowledge" (Hos. 4:6).

Jehovah was speaking about the Israelites, but there could be no truer statement about the Lord's church today – many are led astray and their souls are destroyed because of their lack of knowledge.

Peter says we are to add "knowledge" (2 Pet. 1:5) as a trait that is desirable. We are to "grow in the grace and knowledge of our Lord and Savior Jesus Christ" (2 Pet. 3:18). Peter denied Christ three times. Of all men who could speak to the things that prevent apostasy, Peter is imminently qualified. He says we need knowledge to the extent it is ever increasing.

God desires "all men to be saved and to come to the knowledge of the truth" (1 Tim. 2:4), but we must expend the effort to learn. God, in His wisdom, could have created the written word in a format that was different. It could have been given to us as a list of laws. He could have simplified it even more than it is – but God chose to give it to us through the letters and writings of various inspired men. It is up to us to read, learn, and know what God has said. Knowledge doesn't just happen – it must be grown through much effort. Some are more willing to expend effort on learning a craft (sewing), a sport (golf), or a hobby (playing an instrument) than they are willing to expend on Bible study. What a sad reality.

In our society if a person wants to become a lawyer or doctor we require a great degree of study and knowledge that can be demonstrated before we allow him to enter the profession. This knowledge is important for him to fulfill his responsibilities and function as the office requires. Yet, the average person who claims to be a Christian has engaged in such little Bible study he cannot name the books of the Bible, much less find a passage without help. Do we in the church have a similar attitude in regard to our study? Based on the amount of time we spend learning about godliness, how important is it to us to grow in the knowledge of God?

Religious writing has become very popular in the United States with many books making top 10 lists every year. Many Christians are reading these books and may be influenced by them (to some extent). Closer to home are the religious journals written by conservative brethren, like *Truth Magazine, Focus Magazine*, or *Biblical Insights*. There is some benefit from reading these publications, but do we spend more time on these publications than in God's word? Do we prefer these to God's word? Do we implicitly "trust" these writers or do we weigh their words against the Bible? There is a great danger that we become knowledgeable about what men say, but not about God's word! God's word "is truth" (John 17:17) and the writings of men should not take precedence – even, and especially if, from brethren we feel we can trust.

A thorough history of the Israelite's dealings with God is necessary to understand many aspects of the New Covenant, including the books of Romans and Hebrews. Knowledge of the stories and examples aid in making application to our own lives. Without application, knowledge serves no purpose. The application of knowledge is wisdom. Satan loves nothing more than for Christians to be lacking in knowledge, for then they are that much easier to lead astray. Let us determine to know God's will and apply it to our lives.

Now, Think...

1. Read Romans 1:21-22. What causes some to turn away from the knowledge of God?

2. Read 2 John 10-11. What danger is involved if we do not have sufficient knowledge of the truth?

3. Is study enough (2 Tim. 3:7)?

For Discussion

1. What is the problem of having zeal but not according to knowledge (Rom. 10:2)?

2. What positive attitudes will lead us to grow in knowledge?

   A. Psalm 1:3

   B. Acts 17:10-11

3. From 2 Timothy 3:16-17, provide at least three major points regarding knowledge and study.

   A.

   B.

   C.

4. What part does preaching play in providing knowledge?

5. Are there any books other than Scripture that truly aid our study?

Satan's Victim

1. Describe the attitude of an older (adult) Christian who never or seldom studies.

2. What prevents us from growing in knowledge as we should?

Lesson 13

Satan's Assault On The Faith

Materialism

We live in a very wealthy society. If you have more than one pair of shoes, many in the world would consider you wealthy. Most of us have enough clothes we could go almost a month or more without wearing the same thing. We have homes, autos, an abundance of food, insurance, and financial stability. Sadly, many American Christians do not feel wealthy, and they fail to apply scriptural teachings about the dangers of wealth.

American culture, to a large extent, promotes and encourages the love of money. Many believers have adopted the mind-set that 'I should not be content with what I have,' and that 'I need to get more or get something better.' This attitude toward life leads many into problems with debt, envy, overworking, marital trouble, and loss of faith. When we adopt the attitude of our society, rather than the will of God, we should expect nothing but problems.

In the parable of the soils, Jesus teaches about "the ones on whom seed was sown among the thorns; these are the ones who have heard the word, but the worries of the world, and the deceitfulness of riches, and the desires for other things enter in and choke the word, and it becomes unfruitful" (Mark 4:18-19). How many Christians can be described as being worried about their personal finances? How many have the desire for other things? Some Christians will labor for hours over their checking account, but will not read their Bible for twenty minutes. Some are more studious of the stock exchange report than of the teachings of Christ.

Riches are deceitful in that we think wealth solves our problems. It does not. It brings more issues into our life. By these attitudes toward wealth Jesus says we become "unfruitful." We do not bear the fruit of the spirit which is "love, joy, peace, patience, kindness, goodness, faithfulness, gentleness, self control" (Gal. 5:22-23). The evidence of the Spirit living in us is lacking when our focus is on material things.

The love of money causes some to wander away from the faith (1 Tim. 6:10). Wandering is like drifting–it happens before you notice. You look up and suddenly realize you are not where you thought you were. We then realize the most awful effect of the love of money–we stop loving God. By this we "pierce ourselves with many griefs" (1 Tim. 6:10). We bring these sorrows upon ourselves. We, in essence, stab ourselves in the heart, killing our love for God so that we can love money.

Matthew 19:23-24 has Jesus warning us "it is hard for a rich man to enter the kingdom of heaven. Again I say to you, it is easier for a camel to go through the eye of a needle, than for a rich man to enter the kingdom of heaven." Most Americans do not consider themselves rich, whereas most other cultures in the world would see most of us as rich. We would be wise to pay attention to Jesus' teaching. He says a rich man can be saved "with God" (Matt. 19:26), but it is still hard.

Have we deceived ourselves? Do we think we are righteous when, in fact, we have a love for money? Satan assaults us as Americans with all sorts of temptations and wrong attitudes in regard to wealth. He wants nothing more than to cause us to stumble and fall away from the living God. Materialism is "a preoccupation with or stress upon material rather than intellectual or spiritual things" (*http://www.merriam-webster.com*). God expects us to set our minds "on the things above, not on the things that are on earth" (Col. 3:2).

Now, Think...

1. Read Luke 12:15-21.

   A. What is the proper attitude toward possessions (Luke 12:15)?

   B. What IS life all about (in context)?

2. Read 1 Timothy 6:5-11.

   A. Explain how some think godliness is a means of gain. (1 Tim. 6:5)

   B. Why is contentment important (1 Tim. 6:6-8)?

For Discussion

1. How is man's wisdom different from God's in regard to wealth and material things (Prov. 23:4-5)?

2. Is it better that we be poor (Prov. 11:4; 11:28; 15:16)?

3. How do we learn to be content (Phil. 4:12-13)?

4. Describe some of the "temptation," "snares," and "foolish and harmful desires" when we "want to get rich" (1 Tim. 6:9).

Satan's Victim

1. How do we move away from materialism to a proper Christian mind-set (1 Tim. 6:11-12)?

2. What is to be the Christian's focus and purpose in life (1 Tim. 6:17-19)?

3. How does Hebrews 13:5-6 help the one struggling with materialism?

CPSIA information can be obtained
at www.ICGtesting.com
Printed in the USA
BVHW041200210719
553651BV00010BB/31/P

9 781584 273851